Advance Praise for *Stompin' at The Grand Terrace*

A beautiful tale of friendship built upon old-school jazz and blues in Chicago of the '50s. *Stompin' at The Grand Terrace* is a remarkable document—history, race, music, and love all flow from Philip Bryant's brilliant, jazz-fueled poems.

— Adrian C. Louis, author of *Skins* and *Evil Corn*

Stompin' at The Grand Terrace is destined to be a classic, like those well-worn jazz records the book's speakers, James and Preston, love so much, snapping their fingers, nodding along with the beat. When James and Preston talk, they're always listening to the music, but we get to hear both—the jazz they love and their own righteous arguments about which musician is the best. Phil Bryant not only summons up Ellington, Tatum, Prez, and Bird, he also gives us the heart and soul of his times, from Chicago's South Side to Southern Minnesota—a journey that starts on an impeccable, sustained note and cooks all the way through.

— Joyce Sutphen, author of *Naming the Stars*

Phil Bryant tells stories when he writes poems, and, oh, what marvelous stories he tells in *Stompin' at The Grand Terrace*—stories about his favorite jazz players, stories about friends and family members, stories about the big and little experiences of life, all of them filled with passion and joy, with humor and anger, with wisdom and courage.

I like the sense of urgency in *Stompin'*. The poems scream, "Read me. I have something important to say." And I do read them, all of them, some more than once, some many times. Bryant is the real deal, one of the most spirited and gifted poets writing today.

— Dave Etter, author of *Alliance, Illinois*

Phil Bryant's elegant poems are nothing less than love letters to the men and women who came before us, soulful responses to the call that nurtured a generation. These poems sing from the page with an energy that echoes the great musical artists they celebrate: *Stompin' at The Grand Terrace* is a powerful and important book.

— David Haynes, author of *The Full Matilda*

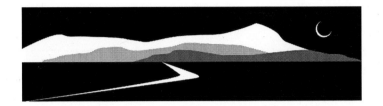

Blueroad Press

2009

Stompin' at The Grand Terrace

Stompin' at
The Grand Terrace

a jazz memoir in verse

Philip S. Bryant

Blueroad Press
Janesville, Minnesota
2009

Blueroad Press
34402 15th Street
Janesville, Minnesota 56048

www.blueroadpress.com

John Gaterud, Editor & Publisher
Abbey Gaterud, Associate Editor

Book and cover design: Abbey Gaterud
Cover photograph © Sasha Radosavljevich

Grateful thanks for permission to reprint the following
quotations and photographs:
Lester Bowie quote: Revolution, No. 1032, November 28, 1999. RCP
Publications, Chicago. Reprinted with permission.
Thelonious Monk quote: From saxophonist Steve Lacy's "Notebook" and
Foreword in *Thelonious Monk: His Life and Music*, by Steve Fitterling (revised
1997). Berkeley Hills Books, Albany, California. Reprinted with permission.
Grand Terrace photographs: University of Chicago Special Collections,
John Steiner Collection, Jazz Archive.

In memory of my father
and the music he loved

Contents

3. Stompin' at The Corner Lounge: 75th & King Drive and Beyond

A Brief Jazz Who's Who

Jazz is neither specific repertoire nor academic exercise…but a way of life.

—Lester Bowie

Let's *lift the bandstand!!*

—Thelonious Monk

GRAND TERRACE CAFE

35th STREET ★ **NEAR SO. PARKWAY**

Postcard: Chicago, 1940

Writing from train station. We'll get there before you get this.
Wonderful honeymoon. Lots of sights. Grand Terrace Ballroom last
night. Saw Andy Kirk & His 12 Clouds of Joy. Marvelous! Colored
couples dancing! Whites stopped and just watched. Simply defied
gravity! By end of night, nobody on floor but colored. Didn't seem
to mind—were half the show and seemed to know it. Kay liked sax
player John Williams. Played beautifully. Asked for his autograph—
hicks in the Big City! Ha! Was good sport, wrote "Best of Luck!
John" on cocktail napkin. Saw Wrigley Building today, so chalky
white. More colored here than I've ever seen. Hi to all! *Wish you
were here!!* See ya soon!

The Grand Terrace Café (also known as the Ballroom) was one of America's premier jazz venues in the early-to mid-twentieth century—an integrated "black and tan" club on Chicago's South Side, where blacks and whites could freely mingle while listening and dancing to some of the greatest musicians in jazz history. Along with its predecessor, The Sunset Café (1917-1928), the Terrace played host to innumerable upstarts and stars, including Louis Armstrong, Cab Calloway, Bix Beiderbecke, Benny Goodman, Charlie Parker, Dizzie Gillespie, Sarah Vaughn, Nat "King" Cole, Teddy Wilson, Billy Eckstine, and Art Tatum. Starting in 1928, legendary pianist Earl "Fatha" Hines led the house orchestra for nearly a dozen years. His band played three—and sometimes four—shows a night, and live radio broadcasts of Hines from the Terrace were regularly heard coast to coast. The Terrace had two locations: at 3955 South Parkway until 1937, then at 315 East 35th Street until 1950, when it closed. The building housing the Grand Terrace on 35th still stands in the Black Metropolis-Bronzeville Historic District, and in 1998 received Chicago Landmark status. _____

Prologue: Stompin' at The Grand Terrace

Picture two black Chicago working-class men living on the South Side of the city just after the midway point of the last century, slowly but steadily easing their way into middle age. They are part of that vast post-war army of working men and women who labored at the various factories, steel mills, slaughterhouses, auto plants, and other blue-collar industries that paid relatively well, but demanded grit, muscle, and endurance. Their class and race permanently marked their status, designated largely by an outside (white) world that surely welcomed their muscles and backs, but otherwise disdained and relegated them to the strict and closed confines of their ethnic and racial ghettos. The ghetto largely and at times narrowly defined the men and women who dwelled there. How they passed their time; what deep thoughts, hopes, dreams, visions, and aspirations they had; what lives they led; and what music they created, played, and listened to went mostly unnoticed and was usually dismissed as having little or no consequence or significance for the wider world that lay just beyond the borders of the ghetto. But for them, their Blues, Gospels, and Jazz were vital and of utmost importance, as seen here through these two aging African American men: Chicago Southsiders fated to a mostly obscure workaday life, trying to eke out a living in order to take care of families, wives, and children, while at the same time striving to kindle and nurture a deeper and more passionate sense of their own inner lives and the immediate worlds they inhabited— which for them was defined, expressed, and reflected in the jazz they collected, listened to, and loved. Music was their haven and oasis, for better and for worse. It gave them (if ever so briefly) a true sense of who they were as human beings. It affirmed a spirit flowing within and between them and throughout the world where they lived and would soon depart and vanish from forever. This spirit they rarely tried to articulate in words or speak of directly. But both men believed in it, in the same way they believed in the music they heard. This is the story of James and Preston—friends, confidants, and companions— in whose dark faces reflects this light and life, lifting and spinning and shining ever forth like music itself across the infinite. _____

1. Stompin' at The Grand Terrace

The Shape of Jazz to Come

Preston came from
work at the steel mill
one afternoon to our place.
My father was playing
Ornette Coleman
The Shape of Jazz to Come.
Preston hated avant-garde
jazz and made no bones
about saying it.
"What is that shit, James?
Tell me. You're an
educated man and I can't
claim to be a scholar
of nothin' but runnin'
that muthafuckin' crane
out there on 91st and South Chicago
but can this nigga play—or
can't he? Is this music?
It's all turned 'round
backwards. *This is the new shit?*
Shit, somebody's tryin'
to unload a whole lotta bullshit on you!
Like all these self-proclaimed
prophets sayin' the same
shit Diz and Bird
was sayin' twenty years ago.
Tell me, James. How can you improve
on somethin' The Rabbit did way
back in 1930?
Sayin' they don't
want to play that way
no more 'cause it's passé.

'Xcuse my muthafuckin' French but
if it's so passé why can't
their black asses play it so it
sounds like somethin' other
than a constipated chicken
tryin' to take a shit?"

My father argued,
"Preston, this is a different time.
Like Bird, Diz, and Monk before them,
Ornette, Eric, and Cecil Taylor
can't play the same way
as their predecessors. They have
to find their own way
—their *own* voice—
that's the genius of jazz."
Preston, shocked,
shot back,
"James, how can an educated,
thoughtful, intelligent man like you
say that a motherfucker
who don't know the first thing
about playing his instrument
is a damn genius? Shit, I guess
I'll just have to shrivel up
and die! Fuck, music ain't
music no more, just some crazy
motherfucker blowin' whatever
shit comes to mind—
don't matter 'bout
notes, chords, playin' in tune or
in time
—*just be a genius*—

and you don't even
have to know one
fuckin' thing about music."

"Cecil Taylor went to Julliard,"
my father said.
"Well," Preston replied,
"they shoulda kept his
no-playin' black ass there at Julliard.
If they think
that's music then
the white boys is more worse
off than I thought."
My father sighed,
took Ornette off,
and put on
Ellington 55, with Paul Gonsalves.
Preston took a long
drag off his beer,
lit up a Pall Mall,
and leaned back on the sofa.
A smile slowly appeared on his face
the way dawn slowly
breaks on a cool autumn morning.

"You must've had
a bad day," my father said.
Preston looked right at him.
"James, you amaze me.
You must be telepathic.
I had a terrible day,
and Ellington was exactly
what I wanted to hear."

My father snorted,
"Well, you just should have
said so then."
Preston closed his eyes.
Gonsalves was into his solo on
Mood Indigo.

"I did."

Swinging Hard

It was snowing so hard outside you could barely see the houses across the street—a thick, heavy, wet snow that sounded like gravel being thrown against the windows. Preston and my dad were having a fierce argument over which pianist could swing harder: Kenny Drew or Hank Jones. Drew was on, playing his part on *Blue Train*. My father said, "You can't tell me Jones ever dreamt of swinging this hard, much less playing it." Preston waved him off. "Shit, James, anybody who plays with Trane is bound to swing hard. Trane would *make* 'em swing. Hell, my grandmother could swing behind Trane, Mr. PC, and Philly Joe." My father said, "And your grandmother could probably jam a lot harder with The Drew than Jones." Preston shook his head, called him out. "Jones is a lyricist," he said. "He ain't in there sweatin' in the kitchen tryin' to cook no collard greens and ham hocks. He don't have to. His playin's more like a Cuban cigar and French cognac after a fine meal." My father walked to the window and watched the snow piling up on the street. Trane had started his solo on *Moment's Notice*. "Cognac or no cognac," he said, "the essence of jazz is to swing, so whether you're cooking French cuisine or black-eyed peas and cornbread, somebody's got to be in the kitch—" but then stopped. "Hey, Pres, we better go out there and see if we can dig your car out." Preston got up and peered through the glass at the snow fallen nearly a foot since they'd started playing records earlier that day. "Damn, it's a muthafucka out there!" He gathered up his records, and both of them put on their coats and boots and went downstairs. My father stood behind the car, pushing while Preston gunned the accelerator, spinning his wheels in the deep snow. "Rock it back and forth," my father hollered. "Ease up a little, then push it down." Preston did, and after a lot of rocking and grunting, the car finally started to free itself from the curb. "Yeah, now swing it hard!" he shouted, and Preston's Corvette fishtailed out into the street. As it started to pull away, my father laughed and yelled, "Yeah, you played that just like Drew— swinging hard! If you'd done it like Jones, you'd still be spinning your wheels!" Preston beeped his horn, flashed his lights, and slowly slid down the snow-packed street.

Radiator Dance

I heard my father tell Preston
the story about seeing Miles' group
with Hank Mobley, Philly Joe Jones,
and Ron Carter at the London House.
In the restroom between sets
he saw Miles on top of the radiator.
Miles Davis, up there,
dancing with his eyes closed.

Not one to miss a beat
my father stepped in.
"What's happ'nin', Miles?"
Miles stopped, mid-stride,
looked down at my dad as if
recognizing an old friend, said,
"Hey! What's happ'nin?"
and went on with his radiator dance.

My old man went over
to the urinal, finished,
and on his way out said,
"Later, Miles."
Again Miles stopped,
looked down, said,
"Later,"
and continued dancing
on the hissing radiator as my father
went out the door.

Irreconcilable Differences

"Yeah," my father said to Preston,
"you remember when Miles was playing
the Nickel a few years back
and he had his group
—arguably his best—
Herbie, Wayne, Tony, Ron."
Preston took a long pull
on his Miller High Life.
"Yeah, he launched all them
bad muthafuckas like they was
in a music conservatory or somethin'.
They was all young turks then."
"Young turks, *nothing*," my father said.
"I saw them go into *Stella*
and Wayne takes a chorus. Miles stops
the whole goddamn band right in the
middle of Wayne's solo
breaks it right
off.
Everyone is stunned. You could hear
a damn needle drop.
And Miles turns to Wayne
—Wayne Shorter, mind you—
and says
Don't play it that way,
muthafucka, play it this way
and proceeds to play Wayne's chorus.
When he stops, Miles tells the band
to pick it up on such and such a chord
on the beat
and then they come in
right on the beat!
as if nothing happened."

They both sat back, took long
pulls of Miller. Miles' version of
Someday My Prince Will Come
spun on the turntable.
Finally, Preston said, "You know,
James, I love Miles
with all my heart, but he can be
one evil muthafucka at times.
Glad I wasn't up there on that stage.
Shit, if I was Shorter,
I woulda put my foot all the way
up that little black muthafucka's ass."
My father said, "Oh, that's just Miles."
Preston said, "I don't care if he's
Jesus of Nazareth. If he pulled
that shit with me on stage
genius or no genius
I woulda kicked his black ass—
or else he'd woulda kicked mine."
"Guess that's why you're not
playing tenor sax in his band!"
They both laughed.
"Yeah," Preston said to my father,
"what do they call it when man and wife
are beatin' the hell out of each other and
file for divorce? What is that?
Irreconcilable Differences?"
"Yeah," my father said,
"I like the sound of that."

Preston's Dream: Version No. 1

Preston came over one Saturday afternoon
with his usual six-pack of Miller
and armful of records. He was in a quiet
pensive mood—almost doleful.
My father caught on and started playing
some Billie Holiday.
"How'd you know I was thinkin'
about Billie?" Preston asked.
"I don't know," my dad said. "A hunch, I guess."
They listened to
Billie's version of *The Way You Look Tonight.*
Billie's version of *Pennies From Heaven.*
Billie's version of *I'll Never Be the Same.*
Finally, Preston said,
"These are all Billie's songs, you know.
She coulda written 'em herself.
In fact, I think she just took 'em
hokey and corny as they are
'cause nobody wanted 'em anymore.
Like in slavery days, the slaves
gettin' pigs' ears, snouts, feet, guts
—all the pieces
the massa felt beneath him to eat—
and makin' 'em into delicacies.
She mined songs,
got the diamonds in 'em that
nobody cared for or knew how to get.
She got it.
Re-created these songs into her own.
She adopted them.
They were all her children,
and they all called her Mama.
Because she was."

My father drank a little beer and smiled.
Billie was singing *Laughing at Life*.
Preston continued.
"I had the strangest dream last night.
I was in this small Midwestern town, all white,
on the Fourth of July. It was sunny,
and a warm breeze blew the flags aloft.
I was watchin' the parade go down Main Street,
bands playin' *Stars and Stripes Forever*
and floats of all kinds advertisin'
the Jaycees and historical society
and people all dressed up in buckskin and Indian outfits.
I was gettin' nervous
'cause I was the only spot in the crowd,
when here comes the last float in line—
I hear Teddy Wilson playing the opening of
I Can't Give You Anything But Love.
And there
on a float made of white and yellow gardenias
—Billie, in her prime—
big and beautiful and leanin' and singin'
into one of those old-fashioned microphones.
And Prez was there, too—pork-pie hat
and shades and cream-white suit
and Little Jazz Roy Eldridge and Joe Jones
and Walter Page and Ram Rameriz! All of 'em!
I couldn't believe my eyes!
I said to a woman holdin'
a big blond baby boy high
over her head and
bouncin' in time to the music
What year is it? I thought
they're all dead—but there they are!
She didn't say anything,

just nodded and smiled
and kept time to the music.
Then I saw Billie turn as she passed us
and smile at the baby
and throw a white gardenia to the mother.
By this time I was cryin' and wanted to catch up—
the float had almost disappeared down the street,
the crowds were too thick,
I couldn't get through.
Then an old toothless farmer in dirty coveralls
put his hand on my shoulder and said
They're gone now,
but they'll be back next Fourth.
You be sure to come back, son,
you're more than welcome here.
I shook his hand, so dirty and gnarled
and hard from heavy farm work.
I said I would, I *will*—
and then I woke up. My heart was poundin'.
I wondered how I could get back,
but it was only a dream."
Billie was singing *Why Was I Born?*
"Jesus, Preston, that was some dream."
"James, it was like it was real.
Prez, Billie, Joe, Teddy
—all of 'em alive!—
playin' in that hick town somewhere
in the middle of nowhere
on the Fourth of July."

No Greater Love

Preston appeared at the door
with an armful of records,
walked in without saying one hello,
pulled a record out of the sleeve,
put it on the AR belt-driven turntable
—it was Eddie Lockjaw Davis—
and said it was a waste of a
muthafuckin' three dollars.
"Listen to that muthafucka!
Honks like a damn goose just flew up
into a bunch of high-tension wires or somethin'.
Went to see the muthafucka
last night down at the Nickel.
He was with Shirley Scott,
and they blew holes *all over*
that establishment
till the white folks got up and told 'em
Now, Jaws, you just tone it down a little
—this here's a respectable place—
ain't no juke joint down on the South Side.
They just laughed. He and Shirl was *cookin'!*
So they go into the sweetest, most soulful
No Greater Love.
Had them white folks from
the Gold Coast shoutin' *Amen!*
Just like niggers after that.
So I take my ass out of bed early this morning,
still on Cloud Nine from last night's performance,
go over to Polk Brothers,
and get this album 'cause it has
No Greater Love.
Boy, what a difference a day makes, James.

Listen to that.
You want it?
You can have it."
Daddy and Preston listened to a syrupy,
uninspired Jaws, minus Shirl Scott,
makin'-a-date, so to say,
just picking up a paycheck.
"*No Greater Bullshit!*
is what they should have called it,"
my father said, finally taking it off the turntable.
"No, Preston, it's yours.
You can keep it."

Stompin' at The Grand Terrace

My father was playing something by Earl Hines—old—probably from the early '30s, when he was still with Louis Armstrong. He mentioned the old Grand Terrace Café, where Hines and the great ones used to play. Preston was snapping his fingers and nodding along with the beat. "That reminds me of a dream I had the other night. It was beautiful, man, in the sense of lights and music. Fatha Hines and Satchmo was *burnin'*. Outside, a soft glow from the streetlights seemed like a Canadian sunset, while inside the crystals of the great chandelier were lit up like a thousand stars. Bean took a chorus. Then Prez. Then Bird. Then Diz. Art Tatum was there. Teddy Wilson, Bill Basie, Lady Day, Don Byas, Duke Ellington, and Baby Dodds. Big Sid Catlett and Little Jazz Roy Eldridge himself. Everybody was diggin' it. People were dancin', not to show off, but to put into movement what the musicians were playin'. Everyone was there. You were there, James, with all these egghead-lookin' white cats. They weren't lookin' too hip, but could somehow dig it. The place got more crowded. You said, *Look, Preston, it's Bach, Beethoven, and Brahms returned from the dead to check out the scene!* I turned and saw these cats in gray powdered wigs, all steadily diggin' the show. Pops and Fatha kicked it into high gear. The place became so crowded I went onto the terrace to get some air. A cool breeze was blowin' as music poured out the doors into the night. People were dancin' on the terrace now, and it began to shake and vibrate. I thought, *Oh, shit, this muthafucka's about to crumble!* And it was a long way down, too—certain death if you fell. Then there was this big crackin' sound, and I thought, *Well, that's it.* We began to list like the *Lusitania* or *Titanic*, and I shouted, *We're all goin' down together!* And then a miraculous thing happened—the music swung that much harder! Pops and Diz were approaching the stratosphere on the bandstand! We righted and were lifted up by the sound. We were saved! The music held us up, James! And that's when I woke up." My father reset the needle on the Fatha Earl Hines album. This time they listened and did not speak.

History

They were listening to Billie Holiday. Preston was agitated about something, but didn't say anything until the record—*Why Was I Born?*—had finished.

"What's the matter now?" my father asked.

"History," Preston said.

"History?"

"Yeah, history. How they write history and leave out things 'cause they don't feel it affects 'em. Well, it does, James."

"What's that got to do with Billie?"

"Everything," Preston said. "First, they screw up tellin' her life story in *Lady Sings the Blues*. That skinny matchstick of a girl, Diana Ross, couldn't sing the blues if you gave her four tablespoons of it a day for the rest of her life! There she is, a real weepin' willow, gnashin' her teeth and drippin' mascara all over the ends of the earth. This is supposed to be Billie? First of all, Billie was no victim. She was a big strong woman who, if she had to, would tell you to kiss her big black ass in whatever place she chose for you to kiss it—*she would!*—monkey or no monkey on her back, you dig. But then they chose to leave out Prez, Teddy Wilson—the great Teddy Wilson—Buck Clayton, Red Allen, all these great men who collaborated with this great artist to make enduring music."

"Preach, now!" my dad shouted, holding up his sixteen-ounce Country Club Malt Liquor, as if to toast.

Preston got embarrassed and fell back into his chair. "Well, I get that shit from hangin' around your bookworm ass, James."

They laughed. Billie was now singing *All of Me*. Prez, on sax, was pushing her out there as far as she could go. Billie, in turn, was giving back as much as he dished out.

"Listen," Preston said, "Billie and Prez together. No one remembers that!"

But they both did.

Confession on Lionel Hampton

Preston blew hot and cold about Lionel Hampton.
"Now, I bopped and hopped to Hamp's band
back in my misspent youth, Lindy-hoppin' with
the best of 'em. He was my main man 'fore I
was all the way into the music,
was just a teenybopper and jive-ass jitterbug.
Illinois Jacquet would send me into orbit
as he gathered his flock to fly all the way home.
I mean, I can't erase it all that easily
from my memory.
So I grit my teeth
and 'xcuse Hamp for bein' laid up
with them rich-ass Republican fat cats.
Instead, I look the other way and remember the
heat he stoked when he was in the kitchen
just plain cookin' and burnin',
the warm lovely down-home smell of his music
like it's Thanksgiving or Christmas come early,
even in the middle of July.
And that ain't no lie.
After that, I can honestly confess:
Later, Lionel, for the rest."

Who Else?

My father threw a litany
of alto saxophonists at Preston:
    Paul Desmond
        Ain't Shit
    Sonny Criss
        Ain't Shit
    Eric Kloss
        Ain't Shit
    Jackie McLean
        Ain't Shit
    Cannonball Adderley
        Maybe—but still
        Ain't Shit
    Phil Woods
        Ain't Shit
    Sonny Stitt
        Ain't Shit
So who else, then? my father asked,
exhausted and just a little put out.
Well, Preston smiled, there's
        Johnny Hodges
    Who Else!

To Tell a Story

My father liked Lee Konitz, but Preston couldn't stand him. "Hell, he sounds like a nuclear physicist scratchin' one of them theorems on a blackboard. Might be brilliant watchin' it unfold, but damn if it's ever gonna move anybody. Though it might blow up a whole lotta folks."

My father shook his head. "Lee's got something to say. It's just on a different frequency than you're used to hearing."

Preston laughed. "James, I don't think my radio can pull in any stations from outer space!"

"Now you're thinking of Eric Kloss."

"Look, all them boys is the same—technically proficient—but when I come in the door, I want to smell the turnip greens and ham hocks a-cookin'. You can do anything you want with the music, but it's got to swing. And you got to tell a story."

"What if it's a story you never heard before?" my father asked.

"And what sad-assed story haven't I heard? A nigga's woman done left 'im? Nigga done lost his damn job, house burned down, and car repossessed? Nigga come home, find his best friend layin' up with his old lady, eatin' his cornbread and greens? Shit, it's as old as time itself— all the way back to the Greeks and Romans, all the way back to the Bible, to Cain and Abel. *Shit, Cain said, how the fuck do I know where Abel is? I ain't lookin' after his raggedy ass!* Man, it's the oldest story in the book. And I done heard most of 'em."

"You must get tired of hearing the same old sad story, then."

"Yes and no," Preston said. "Depends on how someone tells it. Prez tells it so I can listen to it over and over again. Lee Konitz tells it like he's tryin' to explain to his teacher why he ain't got his paper in on time, like the dog ate it or some lame shit like that."

"Oh, you're just a classicist, that's all. You can't stand anything new."

Preston glowed with the flush of holding his own and even besting my father in an argument. "James, if it ain't broke, don't fix it. If anyone can improve on the Sistine Chapel, then you bring 'em to me. Same goes for Prez on *Lady Be Good* or *Dickie's Dream* or *Topsy*. Prez tells a story on each one of those cuts. Not playin' just to be playin'. Prez plays 'cause he's got somethin' important to say."

"Okay, okay," my father said. He got up and took Konitz off the player and put on Lester Young's *I Cover the Waterfront*.

Preston beamed. "Thank you, Brother James, for lettin' me have this one—which don't come often, arguin' with you. May I implore you to hear the sound of the water on the wharf, the fog settin' in, the sound of the ships hittin' their foghorns. And we're just on the first page, mind you."

As Lester blew.

Saving The Trumpet Kings

Preston worked at the steel mills and made good money at the time, was twice married and divorced, paid alimony and child support, and with the rest of his money bought records, hi-fi equipment, and brand-new Corvettes—which, like his marriages, he would then proceed to wreck. My father said he drove like a lunatic, and had vowed never to get in or near a car that Preston drove. One day, he came over with one record instead of his usual armful and with head and hands bandaged.

"What happened?" my father asked.

"They burned up when I went into a viaduct trying to avoid some fool in front of me. (Everyone—*else*—on the road was a *fool*.) I was all right, but the gas tank ignited, and the whole car caught fire. The police came by the time I remembered I'd left my records in the trunk. Only managed to get one—this rare Emarcy release of *Rex Stewart and The Trumpet Kings*. Ran back, put my hand in the blazin' car, got the keys, opened the trunk, and rescued it. Police just about locked me up.

"*Boy, yer crazy! Yer brand-new Vette is burnin' up, and all you can think about is a damn phonograph record! Well, I've seen it all.*

"And I knew then and there how that story would be goin' 'round in some cop bar in Cicero later that night:

"*Yeah, Joe, this crazy nigger went back into his burnin' Vette to get some damn record album. And you wonder why they don't have nuttin' to shake a stick at.*

"Nothin' but this." Preston slowly pulled the plastic off the record jacket, obviously in pain with his bandaged fingers.

"Will you be all right?" my father asked, really concerned.

"Oh, yeah. Once you open me a beer and put on The Trumpet Kings."

Move

This is how I saw them on that faithful Saturday morning. It was bright and cold, a foot of snow on the ground, the sun a bright nickel in the sky. Preston put on *Move*, a tune by Denzel Best, with Sonny Criss, Wardell Gray, and Dexter Gordon. Was more a command than a title, the bebop version of General Patton leading his tanks.

Preston jumped off the couch. "Listen to Criss. Hardly knows how to get 'round the changes, blowin' all them notes like rabbit punches in the late rounds. Each punch lands, but they got nothin' on 'em. Damn, if he don't sound like a boxer staggered and just fightin' from goin' down. Listen!" My father nodded and smiled.

"Now dig Wardell," Preston said. "Like he's comin' in like the grandmaster. He looks over Criss' shoulder and sees he's almost checkmated. Move bishop to rook's pawn—damn! Criss sees it. An opening!"

Preston got closer to the speaker. "Now I hear Dexter talking. Like *Damn, Wardell, don't hog it all—save some for me.* Here Criss wasted his share on the floor. *Now I got to get a taste!* Yeah, that's sweet." My father pointed to Preston, who moved closer still.

"Now here's Dexter goin' out of Jacquet, dressed like Prez. There it is! Damn! Listen to that muthafucka kick. Prez outta Jacquet, you hear that?" He smiled. "That's why they call him Long Tall Dexter—Fastest Gun in the West!"

My father rose, picked up an invisible tenor, and played along with Gray through the next few choruses—riding into the sunset.

Preston winked. "Dexter done told Wardell to move…Your Butt… MOVE…Your Fanny…MOVE…Your Ass…MOVE!"

Liver & Onions: The Pianists

My father was alone.
Preston was supposed to come,
but sometimes without a prior call
wouldn't show.

My father had the weekly selections
picked out—piano players today.
He started at their regular time,
drinking malt liquor and playing
Unit Structures by Cecil Taylor.

My mother, meanwhile,
hated Cecil's music and hated Preston more.
She was furiously chopping up onions
into a skillet of frying calf's liver.

"Liver, again?" I protested. She looked up
and flashed a warning flare, pointing
the knife at me. "Don't complain.
Some kids don't even have this to eat."

My father had gone through three of ten
selections he'd picked out. From Cecil
to Red Garland to Kenny Drew. Now
he was playing Tatum's *Humoresque*
—that choppy beginning—
still hoping the doorbell would ring.

Tatum was almost mocking the
classical Dvořák, before he got down to
hard swing.

My dad looked out the window,
then at his watch, and took
another sip of his malt liquor.

The overpowering smell of
frying liver and onions
and my mother's curses
filled the room.

Cook!

They were in the living room one Friday night listening intently to Booker Ervin's *Blue Book* album. Booker's scratchy, big Texas drawl of a solo was in mid-flight when all of a sudden, exactly on the downbeat, Preston shouted, "*Cook!*" James looked startled at first, then smiled and nodded as Booker began to descend the summit he'd just climbed.

I used to love to hear the sound of that word when Preston or my dad would shout it in the middle of *The Sermon* by Jimmy Smith or Rahsaan Roland Kirk's biblical version of *All the Things You Are* or Shirley Scott's appropriately named *Slow Blues in the Kitchen*.

"*Cook!*" my dad would holler in the middle of her funky organ romp late at night, and I'd get a terrible hunger in the pit of my stomach. I thought I smelled my mother's simmering collard greens and ham hocks on the stove, though she'd put away the food from dinner hours ago.

The Terrace: Revisited

Ben Webster was on, playing *Autumn Leaves*.
Preston came into the living room, shaken.
He'd dreamt about The Grand Terrace again.
"It was the night after King was assassinated.
All the musicians were gathered to play a memorial tribute,
but niggers were riotin', burnin', and lootin' all over.
We came outside and said, 'This is no way to remember
Dr. King and his work!' There was this brother carryin' a big
color TV down the street. *Fuck that. This is what's king now!*
Then they started burning down The Terrace!
Reverend King came out of the flaming building
to get them to stop. Told them they were burnin' their own
history, everything that was good about 'em as a people.
One of 'em just pushed him out of the way.
Nigger, you dead. You had your time, now it's our time,
so get out the way!
With that, he lit a Molotov cocktail and threw it into
the already-burnin' building. All the musicians who got out
stood with their instruments and watched it burn. Prez, Bean,
Bird, Duke, Lady Day, Don Byas, Louis, Art Tatum,
Count, Diz, Roy, Rex Stewart, and so many more appeared
in the crowd, watchin' as it burned, as siren and glass broke the air.
After a while, one of Jelly Roll's kin pushed to the front.
It's over now, folks. You can all go home.
The burning Terrace lit up the night sky.
Then I woke up."
My father got up and put on the other side of Ben Webster.
"A sad dream," he said, handing Preston a beer. "A very sad dream,
indeed."

Miles Davis (Slight Return)

Don't play it that way,
muthafucka, play it this way
and then he
played it
and when he did
we all looked at him
audience as well as musicians
as if he were that
little black African
son of a bitch Legba
leading us
farther up a narrow
winding path
that led deep into
a dark wooded hollow
and we had to think
long and hard
for ourselves
if we were brave enough
now to follow.

Miles: Prince of Darkness

I remember my father's stories
about him being cold, fitful,
reproachful, surly, rude, cruel,
unbearable, spiteful, arrogant, hateful.
But then he'd play
Some Day My Prince Will Come
in a swirl of bright spring colors
that come after a heavy rain
making the world anew again
and like the sometimes-tyrannical king
who is truly repentant of his transgressions
steps out onto the balcony
to greet his subjects
and they find it in their hearts
to forgive him for his sins
yet once again.

Rufus Was a Jug Man

Jug is on. *Juggernaut* is playing.
Guess who I saw the other day?
Who?
Rufus.
Rufus! My God, I thought he was dead!
So did I.
Well, what was he doing?
Playin' on a street corner.
You lyin'.
If so, I'm dyin'.
Rufus played with Bird. In fact,
        he damn near cut Bird at Club De-Lisa's
        that night in '52.
I know, I know.
Well, did you say anything to him?
Couldn't. He was playin'.
Well, afterward, then.
Don't think he recognized me.
So you didn't.
Okay, James, I was a little bit embarrassed
        to go up to him, Rufus—the Great Rufus.
        I remember how he was in his prime
        and I'm goin' to go up to him now and say
        Rufus, what's happ'nin'?
So he's scuffling now.
He's playin' out in the streets!
Does he still have that monkey?
Couldn't tell.
Damn, so you just left without
        saying anything to him?
I put a dollar in his case.
A dollar!

That's all I had at the time.

What'd he do?

He nodded and kept on playin'.

How'd he sound?

Like I was listenin' to Jug.

Ole Rufus—he was always a Jug Man.

Always was and always will.

The President

Even though
a cold November rain
blows through the
loose windows of
our third-floor apartment,
Preston is all sunshine and tropics.
He'd come across
a rare Lester Young LP
thrown into the dollar bin
at Polk Brothers, along with
The Ray Coniff Singers,
Mitch Miller Goes Brazilian,
and Bobby Dee's *In the Mood for Romance.*
"I couldn't believe my eyes.
You know, I was just
flippin' through the stacks,
not payin' too much
attention when—*bang!*—
Prez In Sweden jumps out.
Mint condition, not so much as a scratch!
Prez—The President!
One of those rare finds
you live your whole
life for—and imagine, a buck!
I thought I was pullin' off
a great heist, a grand larceny. I was so
nervous, knew the clerk
thought I was up to somethin'.
'Bout ran out of
that store lest somebody say
Come back!
We made a terrible mistake!

But, of course, nobody followed, though
they would've if I'd tried to steal a TV
or sofa. So I slowed down, thinkin'
Shit, I'm actin' like a damn fool!
I'm like that guy in that sci-fi flick,
the last man alive on Earth who
calmly goes down to the museum
to pluck a Rembrandt from its walls
to put up in his penthouse bedroom.
Who's gonna know who
Lester Young is anyway?"
He pops a bottle of Miller.
The rain is turning to sleet,
now hitting hard against the windows.
"I do," my father says,
downing a small glass of whiskey,
"and I want to hear it."
He puts the record on his
Thorens Transcription turntable.
They listen. It's early November 1960.
Election time, Nixon vs. Kennedy.
But when my father
hears Lester's first upturned note,
he smiles a knowing smile
at Preston. "Ahhh!
The President!"

Crazy Rhythm

Preston got up while listening to Coleman Hawkins' solo on *Crazy Rhythm*. "James, Bean just jumped off the stage like he suddenly went crazy. Down on the dance floor, he swept this fine, big-legged chocolate mama off her feet and started dancin' the crazy solo he was just playin'—note for note. You could see it! I mean, everyone saw it and understood it was Bean's solo of *Crazy Rhythm* he just played up on the stand. After the chorus, he kissed the mama on the cheek, thanked her, jumped back on the stage, picked up his horn—and took right up where the band was without missin' a beat. Well, it brought the house down. That's Bean for you. Cool as a cucumber—like nothin' happened at all. After that, everyone waited for him to do it again, but he never did. And the woman he danced with, I never saw her again after that night, either." Preston sat down just as Hawkins played the final notes of *Crazy Rhythm*.

Discovering a New Star: Sonny Stitt

Preston removed
the album's cellophane wrapper.
A bright gem?
A dark, precious sapphire?
He held the unplayed
shiny black diamond
disc carefully between
the palms of his hands.
"James," he said, "I have
just discovered a new star
in the constellation Orion."
He set it on the record changer.
They listened,
charting its exact course
and position in the vast infinite cosmos.
"What shall we call it?"
my father asked as
they heard the fading echo
of a beautiful alto.
Preston looked toward the heavens.
There was absolutely no question.
"We'll call this star
Sonny Stitt."
"Sonny Stitt, it is!"
my father said, reaching
to turn over the record
as if gently adjusting the lens
of a telescope.

Hellhound on His Trail

One Saturday Preston came over all shook up.
"What's wrong, Pres? Looks like the dog done
got ahold of you," my father joked.
Preston laughed. "That's literally the truth."

A big black dog had jumped from behind
a garbage can, snarling with its teeth bared
and crouching to attack Preston, who'd gone out
to the alley to open the garage door.

He dropped his records, picked up a garbage can lid,
and started banging it with his fists and cursing at
the dog at the top of his lungs while he reached for his
shank—a pearl-handled, ten-inch Stiletto switchblade.

"Go on, 'fore I slit you down the middle like a
turkey for Thanksgivin'." The dog backed off a bit,
but still barked and growled, giving little ground.
Preston continued to shout at the mutt,
but could it see was flea-bitten,
wet, cold, and hungry. "Go on outta here, I say!"
The dog lunged and snapped at him.
Preston parried with his knife and garbage can shield.
He looked into the raging yellow and red eyes
of the dog and saw his own image reflected
—crouched, tense, uncertain.

"It was a classic Mexican standoff,
but somethin' came over me,
and I just dropped the lid and put the knife away.
I raised my hands to show him I had nothin' in 'em.
He still growled and watched me,

but didn't try to attack. I said,
Go back where you come from—
ain't no sense in tryin' to kill each other."
Finally, the dog turned and slowly started down
the alley, half-turning back a few times to give
Preston a hard, parting look. And then he
was gone. Preston's hands shook so hard
he could barely pick up his albums.
That's when he came over. My father opened a can
of malt liquor and gave it to him. Preston drank
it down in one long gulp.

"What shall we start with this afternoon?" my father asked.
Preston laughed. "How 'bout Robert Johnson's
Hellhound On My Trail?"
It took a few minutes for my dad to find it
in his few, scattered blues offerings, but he did.
They listened, nodding as Robert Johnson sang,
I got to keep moving, I got to keep moving
Blues falling down like hail, blues falling down like hail
Mnnn, blues falling down like hail, blues falling down like hail
And the day keeps on remindin' me, there's a hellhound on my trail
Hellhound on my trail, hellhound on my trail.

A Case of Mistaken Identity

When Preston came in, James looked at him with concern. "Do you feel all right? You been dreaming again? You weren't dreaming about The Grand Terrace again?" Preston laughed, "No." But something strange had happened, and he didn't know if he should tell my father about it. Popping a couple cans of ale, my dad said, "Oh, come on. The doctor's in, so spill it out."

"You know, James, how I hate the new thing, all that avant-garde shit I think's ruined John Coltrane, Miles, and Ornette Coleman— who wasn't ruined 'cause that nigger couldn't play in the first place. Well, that record of Ornette you gave me, told me to sit down and listen to, said, *Listen! Clear your head of all your petty prejudices!* So I'm your friend and do consider you knowledgeable and probably even the smartest mutherfucker I've ever known—at least a nigger I can talk real shit with, you know, somethin' deeper than pussy, sports, and automobiles. Well, I set down and listen, really listen, like you said, and *Damn!* I can't believe it! I start likin' this no-playin' mutherfucker! Granted, you give me somethin' where he's coverin' a whole lotta old standard tunes. But he's soundin' like, lo' and behold, he can actually play a few of them songs halfway decent with only a few of them honks and squeaks he usually plays on that shit he has the nerve to call *a tune*." Preston leaned back and sipped his ale.

"Maybe you are right, James. Jazz is only what you hear at that moment and for that moment only. For it to really be jazz, it has to constantly change from moment to moment, like the seasons of the year, like the years themselves." My father was bemused—and a little stunned—to hear Preston wax poetic. Then he leaned into the music with his listening ear to the record that Preston had put on. "Wait a minute. Is that the one I gave you?" Preston nodded, Zen-like. Sure enough, the album sleeve said *Ornette Coleman: Goin' Way Back*, but then my father looked at the record on the turntable—*Johnny Hodges: New Horizons.*

"Preston, I'm sorry to say, what I think we have here is a case of mistaken identity," my father said, showing him the album sleeve and Hodges disc. Preston cupped his ears to listen and then broke into a big embarrassed smile. "Shit, that *is* Rabbit, ain't it!"

They listened for a bit. "So," my father said, "I guess it goes without saying that you'll take back every last thing you just said about Ornette and the new thing, right?" Still smiling, Preston said, "Well, Jimmy, my man, you got me. Either my ears ain't as sharp as they used to be—or else your crazy taste in music is startin' to wear off on me a little."

"Good," my father said. "Now let's put on some Jackie McLean." Preston waved his can in the air. "Not so fast, James. Let's finish Hodges. You can't lead the flock too fast to the far pasture, 'cause they might be too tired to eat once they get there." My father, impressed by Preston's poetic analogy, said, "Okay, then, we'll play Ornette later," and put the record down. Preston smiled. "Yeah, later, that's right, James. Make that much later."

As Hodges launched into Ellington's classic, *Sophisticated Lady.*

Swing's Our Thing

On Listening to Them Listen to Hodges and Hines

Open Ears

James! Pass me another forty over here, will ya?

Mean to Me

Yeah, my second wife was so light-skinned, people thought she was white. That ofay judge took one look at her in court and then at me and said, *Nigger, I'm gonna have to give her all yo' damn money.*

Doll Valley

This fine mama had an ass on her so big, James, that I thought I'd need a compass and a map to find my way around it.

Can a Mouse Crochet?

So when my old prejudiced-ass boss asked me if I thought a nigger could do that job, I told 'im *Can a clock tell time? Does snow fall in January? Is there gold in Fort Knox? Can a cow moo? Can a rooster crow? Do fish swim? Do geese fly south in the winter, you white mutherfucker?* Which I wanted to say, but didn't.

One Night in Trinidad

I had some of that shit from the islands he'd been smokin' all night long, just one hit, mind you. Hell, shit 'bout took me outta this world, I mean for good!

Night Train to Memphis

Yeah, it was 1956, and we was going through the Deep South. In the Army, all the brothers on one train. We'd stop in these little-ass country towns. James, let me tell you, thinkin' 'bout all them mean-ass peckerwoods down there, we sho' had our M1 rifles cocked and loaded all the time.

Bustin' With Buster	He's in jail now, doing ten to twenty. Stupid lil' mutherfucker so strung out on shit, tried to rob a damn bank with his son's toy cap gun.
Over the Rainbow	Okay, there's Judy Garland singing it, but have they ever heard the Divine One's version?
Do It Yourself	I don't need nothin' from nobody, James, *'cause I always pays my own way!*
The Cannery Walk	Well, it's ten. Got to walk. Get up in the mornin', chop some mo' cotton for Mr. Charlie out there at U.S. Steel. Later, Jimmy. Remember: Swing's Our Thing. Be seein' you. It's been real!

The Death of Bill Evans

Late 1980, heading north on the Dan Ryan Expressway, just about 35th Street, approaching old Comisky Park. The jazz station I'm listening to reports Bill Evans' death. I remember my father and Preston discussing, back in the late '60s, when cities were burning and Black Power and militancy were in the air, whether whites could—or had the right to—play jazz.

"It's a free damn country," Preston said. "Supposedly people can play whatever they damn well please. White, black, yellow, red, polka dot people—if a mutherfucker can play, he can play. Don't make no difference."

My dad said, "What about the argument that whites are stealing blacks' music, making millions off it while blacks don't get a dime, if that, when they create it?"

"Well, James, that's happened, too. But, practically speaking, what the fuck you gonna do about it? Zoot Sims or Bill Evans shouldn't be put in that boat. Those white mutherfuckas can flat-out play— no ifs, ands, or buts. At the Bee Hive one night on 55th Street, I saw Bill Evans burn it up so much I thought they'd have to evacuate the building 'cause of folks gettin' smoke inhalation. Just blues for the first set, nothin' but blues. Knew he was playin' for some real down-home black folk—and to make a statement sayin', *Dig this—okay?*

"Wasn't 'bout slummin', neither. You know, how some them other smart white boys you listen to sometimes get. No vain-glorious shit like, *I'm white and I can play this black shit, too.* It was just soul-to-soul, you know. *Here it is, ready or not, it's just the blues.* And everyone dug it, knew where he was comin' from, said, *Okay, Bill, relax now, we dig where you at.*

"In the second set, he switched to ballads—*My Foolish Heart, My Romance, Waltz for Debbie*—as if to say, *Here's my real gifts to you. Just to you.* It was fuckin' beautiful. After the set, I went to thank him. Looked like some damn U of C professor, black horn-rim glasses, hair slicked back. We talked about Rabbit, who was one of his favorites. So don't tell me nothin' 'bout race—either a mutherfucker can play or else he can't."

My father had put on Bill Evans' *Peace Piece* while Preston was still talking. Preston had smiled at the memory of meeting Bill Evans. They'd both laughed.

I pass a sign on the freeway: *Detour Ahead*.

Basement Apartment: Blues and the Abstract Truth

My dad did not go to Preston's much. He mostly came to our place. On one occasion, one cold, rainy, gray November afternoon, he invited both of us. He had some old Race records by Duke Ellington to show us. Preston lived in the basement unit of a big apartment house on 80th and Drexel Avenue. He opened the door dressed in a long navy-blue terrycloth robe and black stocking cap—like a Trappist monk letting us in the heavy gate of a secluded monastery. He greeted us, but then apologized for the way his apartment looked. His most recent wife had taken all his furniture in the divorce settlement. He'd meant to clean up, but had worked overtime at the mill, so he was just getting up. The living room and dining room were spartan—couch, coffee table, television set, easy chair. That was it. Fireproof canvas work clothes were piled on the floor. A half-eaten bowl of popcorn sat on the coffee table and could have been there all week. The small kitchen contained a metal table, two chairs, refrigerator, a few dirty dishes in the sink. It looked like a stark motel room where you'd stay only the night, glad to check out first thing in the morning. We passed the first bedroom—a queen-size box and mattress on the floor, covers askew, the walls bare except for a cross over the bed. The room had a small table lamp and an electric alarm clock. We continued down the narrow hallway to the "master" bedroom, where Preston kept his record collection and stereo equipment. There, records on shelves completely took up the four walls of the large room. A conservative estimate would be more than twenty thousand albums. These were broken into fifty or so sections, each meticulously ordered and numbered. A card file cataloged all of them. The section on Johnny Hodges contained nearly 150 albums. The first shelf held old 78 Vocalions of Count Basie and Jimmie Lunceford. Deccas and Columbias, Okeys in original sleeves and in pristine condition. No one had spoken in the inner sanctum. I remember hearing the hum of a dehumidifier and then sinking into the berber carpet. Track lights lit and warmed the room. His stereo system was state-of-the-art—Thorens turntable, Klipsch woofer and subwoofer system, McIntosh amp and pre-amp—housed in a custom-made oak stand. Oliver Nelson's *Blues and the Abstract Truth* lay there. We were in the vaults of the Louvre or The Prado, staring out at the twenty thousand albums—years' worth of American music, culture, and history. Preston, hunched over, looked older and more feeble than his real age. I wondered what would become of all these treasures. His children barely knew him; his wives, he said, were only interested in his money. They'd all told him to keep his goddamn records. We listened to *Lester Leaps In*, a mint-condition 1939 original Vocalian recording of the timeless Lester Young. It sounded as if he might have recorded it the day before. Preston showed us the record sleeve: *Best to you always, Prez, Chicago, August 9, 1951*. Lester leapt while outside an early winter gale blew. Prez was spinning around an infinite black universe on the turntable. The music was perfect, crystal clear, and true.

2. Stompin' With Aunt Janey

Famous Quotes of Aunt Janey

On my grandfather's death:
"The peacemaker's gone, and now this family's going to hell in a handbasket."

On preachers:
"That preacher's so crooked that when he dies and they bury him, they'll have to screw him into the ground."

On hygiene:
"That bitch's butt is so funky she'd draw a swarm of flies in February."

On native intelligence:
"God bless my nephew, Philip. I sent him out for a head of lettuce, and here he comes back with a head of cabbage."

On men:
"All men aren't dogs, but all men got dog in 'em."

On the riots:
"Lord, we aren't ready yet."

On my Afro:
"Boy, somebody needs to put a hot comb through them naps."

On types of people:
"There are only two types of people in this world—the screwers and the screwees."

On God:
"I've tried to be a Christian woman all my life 'cause I know God don't like ugly too long."

On teen pregnancy:

"That's a fast little heifer there; it won't be long 'fore she comes 'round all sad and lost with her belly popped out, and won't be a nigger to be found nowhere."

On white people:

"Philip, let me tell you something: White people's shit don't smell like ice cream, either."

On women's strengths:

"Do you see this (waving a .38 police Special in the air)? This is called The Great Equalizer. This makes me as strong as the strongest man on Earth. As long as I got this, ain't no man gonna be fool enough to lay a finger on me."

On airplane travel:

"I don't like to take no planes 'cause it might not be my time to go, but it might be the pilot's time to go."

On life:

"You do what you have to do, and don't worry about what anybody else says. Remember, one day when they put the last clean white shirt on you and throw that first shovel of dirt on you, it won't be nobody in the casket but you."

Mixing Up of Cornbread

Janey stood over a bowl,
mixing up a batch of cornbread.
"Now the problem with people
trying to understand black folks
is that they take one slice of cornbread,
eat it, either like it or don't,
and then expect the rest of the cornbread
to taste the same as that one slice
they just eaten.
In fact, some folk get so smart
and full of themselves,
they wanna write a whole book
on just that one slice they took,
like they some kind of expert on cornbread.
And they can fool a whole lotta folks that they is,
'cause ain't none of them never had no cornbread
to begin with, either."
She beat harder
with her big wooden spoon.
"Now, Philip, let me tell you something.
There ain't no way that you can tell
what a whole pan of cornbread taste like
by just eating one slice.
In fact, with a really good batch of cornbread,
each slice is gonna taste different
with the same ingredients. Same eggs,
corn meal, milk, butter, salt, bacon-fat grease,
baking powder—all mixed up in the same bowl.
Each slice is gonna taste like itself apart from the rest
no matter how many ways you slice it.
It's a mystery, Philip, even to me.
God don't use no recipe.

He just throws in what he thinks he needs
and don't measure nothing exactly.
It's always approximately a cup, not exactly a cup."
She throws in a handful of corn meal
and beats the batter into a shimmering, smooth,
yellow, warm, perfect sun. It shines high
over us in the noonday summer sky
as if showering a prism of rainbow colors
through broken and splintered glass.

Pot of Greens

And so it comes down
to Janey and me,
a small boy walking with his aunt
hand-in-hand
on crowded State Street
between Washington and Randolph
in the mid-1950s
on a bright cool crisp
autumn day.
The sky
clear blue
when an older white man
dressed in an expensive tailor-made
gray pin-striped suit,
silk tie, leather briefcase
appears out of nowhere
walks by and then turns
to Janey and politely asks
what he could possibly do
for her generously wide hips
and big legs. Whereupon
Janey stops dead in her tracks
looks at the man a long time
up and down
and in a firm tone
that's far from mean
politely smiles and says
"Honey, it don't look like
you got enough there
to season a pot of greens."
She turns from him
taking my hand

and proceeds up State Street
toward Lake
leaving the man
standing there
fuzzy and dazed
literally frozen in her wake
under a clear-blue autumn sky.
He looked like one of those
black-and-white photographs
they used to take in those days.

Two to Tango

Janey was
no great philosopher,
but one day she did
tell my sister,
"A man can
get down in the
gutter, roll around
in the dirt, get up,
brush himself off,
and go on his way
as if nothing happened,
but if a woman gets
down there and gets
dirty, she stays dirty."
Then she
looked over to me,
not to let me off the hook.
"But, Philip,
always remember,
it takes TWO to tango."

Washing Aunt Janey's Feet

I remember Janey in
her pale-blue Fair Store uniform
after a long day's work.
She worked in the kitchen
making homemade pickles
and potato salad
for the store's restaurant.
Coming home, she'd kick off
her shoes and sink into
the easy chair.
Her feet, a tapestry of miles walked
as maid, waitress, cook,
postal clerk, night nurse,
line worker in an English muffin factory,
were as hard and cratered
as the surface of the full moon.
Her toes, like ancient scrolls
of Biblical testaments
written in early Aramaic,
their bones pushing the surface
of the skin like geologic faults,
tectonic plates shifting and moving,
causing slight tremors,
a shudder and shake on the surface
of her dark brown skin.
I'd rub her feet as she'd
close her eyes and moan,
"Lord, have mercy."
And I thought of John the Baptist,
washing the feet of all those tired
laboring souls gathered
to be baptized and anointed.

I'd see her great brown powerful legs
at rest and want to follow them
all the way up. Rubbing, massaging,
and caressing to that dark mysterious
place—still far from me at that young age.
Without opening her eyes, she'd smile,
"Philip, now don't go up too far,
just to my toes for now."
She'd sink back
into her after-work twilight slumber
as I pressed my fingers against her toes,
the very tops of dark hard roots
extending down from an ancient giant oak.

How She Smelled

I used to love
the end of church
services—the big
women crowded toward
the basement rooms,
how the air would be
filled with the smell
of their perfume mixed
with sweat.
Their delicate white
handkerchiefs fluttered
during the sermon
like butterflies above
their brows as they
wiped away beads of
perspiration.
It was a bittersweet smell:
the gentle and
sweet of Janey
bending to kiss me on
my brow as I stood in
the hallway with arms full of
Christmas presents—
how it mixed with
the acrid rancor of the time
she and my grandmother
spoke in lowered tones
so we children would
not hear of a great aunt
recently passed away,
until Janey could no
longer contain herself

and blurted out loud, "No, Belle,
I guess I couldn't
stand that little high-handed
yellow bitch!" The furtive
glances our way as we were turned
out into the freezing cold so the discussion
could continue. Coming in again,
I could smell Janey's perfumed
scent and sweat as she struggled
to get my coat unzipped, her massive body
flexed and tense.

Trouble Down the Line

Janey and my grandmother
were in low tones again.
"That baby is ugly."
"Yes, he is rather homely."
"And no one knows
who the first father is?"
"Uhmmmmmm, huh!"
"And let me tell you
what happened to me,
Belle, when I had to
change that baby once."
Janey moved her face in close—
she was whispering now.
"I undid that baby's
diaper and all of a
sudden his thing
popped out like
a coil of rope—just
like an old snake!
Well, I jumps back and
screamed—about to frighten
me to death. And then here comes
Adrianne with her retarded
self coming in, *What's a matter?*
What's a matter? and I
lie and tell her I'd
seen a roach. She got all
embarrassed and goes back into the
kitchen to get the spray,
comes back,
and commences to spray
all over that child in his crib."

"She didn't!" my grandmother stops Janey.
"Yes, she did, Belle. I'd
never seen anything like it.
I told Adrianne
Stop spraying
that child with bug spray
'cause it's like to deform him!
But when I looked
down and saw him,
I thought it was probably
too late. I tell you, Belle,
it was just as big and long
as an old snake, a child
with something like that."
They paused.
"He's marked for life,
that poor boy, God help him."
"That only trouble down
the line," Janey added.
"Trouble and more trouble
down the line."

White Socks

I remember
Aunt Janey
all in black
standing over the
grave of an older
sister she didn't like
who had
treated her
cruelly when
she was growing up.
Her eyes closed,
head bent, her prayer was, "Laverne,
the Lord has you now.
I hope with those pair
of white socks that you stole from Woolworth's,
which when Mama asked you, you put it on me,
so I got the whuppin'.
This is the last you'll
ever hear it from me."
And then she spat.
And then it started
to rain. And Janey said, raising her black umbrella,
"Hmm, the Lord seems to
know what I'm talking about."
With a smile,
she spoke to the rain-slappered coffin,
"So, you rest in peace now, Laverne."

Rising From the Dead

Uncle Henry,
in one of his religious moods,
shouted out a bit of scripture
at the dinner table,
"And on the third day
He rose from the dead!"
clapped his hands,
and sang, "Alleluia!"
Aunt Janey sat "unmoved"
at the other end of the table,
raised her head slightly,
and said under her breath,
"That's a whole lot more rising
than what Henry did
in bed last night."
Henry, looking over his plate,
wasn't sure what he'd heard.
"What'd you say, Janey?"
She looked innocent
as a newborn lamb
in the manger.
"Why, how should I've known
it would take Him
a whole three days
to rise up from the dead?"
Uncle Henry,
about to quote more chapter and verse,
opened his mouth,
but thought the better of it.

The Death of Uncle Henry

Henry sickened and suddenly
shriveled like a prune.
By the time we visited him in the hospital
the next day, he was dead.
Janey was a stoic through it all.
Held up like a well-built ship in heavy seas.
While others broke and splintered against
the weight of his passing and went under,
she withstood even the would-be scandal
as it unfolded during the funeral service.

No one had known the strange woman
who wept and wailed in the far back pew.
My grandmother held Janey's arm tight
through singing *It's My Cross to Bear*,
and *Abide In Me*, fearing a terrible scene.
Janey scoffed and looked back at the
bereaved woman and then at the coffin
and said loud enough to be heard
by the mystery woman and the room full of mourners,
"I guess every dog has to have her day."

Afterward, after a few straight scotches
and bourbons at the family gathering,
she declared, "I sure won't miss Henry's
snoring none. For thirty-one years
he kept me awake most of the night."

Then, that first night alone, she went right
off into a deep sleep, but was startled awake
by a dream of Henry snoring loudly next to her.
Only when she felt for the first time

in that eerie black silence
the empty space
on the side of the bed
where he had been,
only then did she break down, weeping.

Higher Up He Go

Janey and my grandmother
were in their hushed tones
on the phone. I managed to catch
only the bare bones of what Janey said.
"The nerve to call himself
a preacher—preaching
the gospel of the Lord.
"What he say?
"He didn't!
"And got all those kids himself.
"Well, what did she do?
"You're kidding.
"And he did what?
"Wait a minute—and he's supposed
to be a Christian?
"And what did she do?
"Lord, she didn't!
"Chile, go on.
"The Blood of Jesus!
"And what did his
wife do when she
saw her like that?
"He told her what?
"And she believed him!
"Lord, I guess it takes all kinds
to make a world.
"What kind of hypocrite
could go 'round quotin'
the Bible, chapter and verse?
"She what?
"Good, then that means she's got
a little sense that God gave her.

"So where's he now?
"What? Why that low-down dirty—"
Janey turned around and saw me listening.
"I can't talk so loud, Belle," she said,
motioning her hand in my direction,
then whispered into the receiver,
"Well, you know what they say about
how more of a monkey's ass
shows the higher he climbs up a tree."
I cranked my head out the window,
looked at the big elm tree
in Janey's backyard.
"Philip, what in God's name
are you looking at?"

3. Stompin' at The Corner Lounge: 75th & King Drive and Beyond

All Night Long

He thought it would end with Bobby "Blue" Bland. You know, the slow one. But it didn't. That mellow crooner just gave way to a raucous number by the Delfonics. Completely out of character for them, he thought, with a name like the Delfonics. Well, never mind. Now it's going on three o'clock. Seems the party's not over—or it's just getting its second wind. It's Sunday, for God's sake! Don't these people have to get up in the morning to work? Okay, yeah, they probably don't work. They fit the mode. Never see them early in the morning, only late at night. Car doors slamming, women laughing, footsteps up the stairs and down. He recognizes *Rescue Me* by Fontella Bass, an oldie but goldie. These people must be my age! They should know better. Someone breaks a glass, screams, laughs. Billy Young now. *Have Pity on Me!* Yes, the sadistic bastards must have a sick sense of humor. This is torture! Three-thirty in the morning! A few more hours and he'll be up while they'll be sleeping. The Radiants' *Hold On! I'm coming,* you mutherfuckers! *What About Me?* The Valentines chime. That's it. He takes a broom and starts thumping the handle against the ceiling. Almost exactly to the beat, he hears them dancing, their feet moving back and forth to Barbara Carr's *Don't Knock Love.* He continues banging. Can't they hear him? Now Marlena Shaw, repeating over and over, stuck in the record's black groove, "Mercy, Mercy, Mercy," and then the refrain, "All night long...All night long...All night long... All night long...."

A Night at the Sutherland Ballroom

That night at the Sutherland Ballroom
way back in the mid-1960s,
I caught Cannonball
and Nate Adderley,
with Yusef Lateef.
Redd Foxx opened the show.
Dirty, dirty, and even more low-down dirty
than I ever heard him,
like Cannon can get down on alto
when he's not playing sanctified or
an all-blues or hard-bop groove.
Redd starts riffing on white folks.
"White folks, they like our music,
our dance, the way we talk—
they just don't like us.
That's like orderin' up some spareribs,
coleslaw, and cornbread
and sayin', *Waitress, could you*
hold the niggers, please?"
This is 1965: Selma, Birmingham,
sit-ins, Malcolm dead
only a few short months,
and, of course, Watts.
I'm one of the few white faces in
a sea of black—wave after wave of laughter
lapping up against that distant shore.
Everybody's looking at me.
I'm adrift on this stormy sea
and laugh the loudest and the
hardest of all of them.
Redd says, "Hey, white boy,
what you laughin' at?"

Everything stops. It's so quiet
you could hear lint falling off a suit coat.
I say, my head toward the heavens,
"My people, my people!"
Redd howls, and laughter from everyone follows.
"Boy, you better stay right there, then,
'cuz you're in a whole world of trouble."
Later, though I could have been imagining it,
before playing one of his signature tunes,
Cannon looks straight at me, winks, and smiles.
"This is a new tune, straight up the river
from Arkansas or Mississippi.
We call it *Mercy, Mercy, Mercy*."

City Music

The echo of the wind blowing
through the dark alleyway
is the music of
hardened cement; asphalt
is the black kettle drum
that thumps beyond the melody.
I can see one dark stream
pouring from
a rain gutter.
I can hear
Fat Janet calling
me into a dimly lit
breezeway.
"Not now, not now," she says,
"turn down the music first."
The EL rumbles past.
Turn down the music
a little—the concrete has turned into
a petrified river.
I slip my hand underneath
her dress.
It's like looking for a
tooth under the pillow,
and I don't know what
love is, nor its shape
or feel: only the breeze
through the breezeway,
the music of asphalt and cement,
the snare drum of footsteps,
the rush of rain from a gutter,
and the echo of
the wind blowing
through a dark alleyway.

Delicacy

As a boy I discovered
the origami of chitterlings,
the paper entrails young pigs fold within.
A delicacy! A delicacy!
How strange these native customs were.
I remember Miles playing *Billy Boy.*
The solo trumpet, in 1957,
sounded like the gypsy moth
knife sharpener rolling his
ragtag yellow cart down the
empty midday streets shouting
Sharpens knives! Sharpens knives!
over and over.
This was the first time
I heard a mute sputter that way,
so sharp and dangerous.
I think it was on New Year's Eve.
A pig's head filled with black-eyed
peas and okra cooked for good luck
and sitting on a silver platter
like the head of pale Marie Antoinette
just rolled
off from under a guillotine:
considered then by my people
as still another delicacy.
How strange these native customs were.

Nutty

Monk wrote this
tune *Nutty*
which reminds me of
how I'd act around
Phyllis Lerner because
I had a big crush on her.
I'd make faces,
stand on my head,
yell out her name from way down at
the other end of the block.
She'd say, "Philip is just acting so nutty,"
and "I wouldn't be caught dead with
him if he were the last man on Earth."
Oh, if Phyllis could
hear Monk's tune now,
the way he twists those little nutty chords
into some lovely half-naked Pre-Raphaelite
painting. She wouldn't think
it so nutty
nor would she think it of me, either.

Wade in the Water

I wanted to say
Honey chile', let's dance!
but didn't move
from my place
in that dark corner.
She was a big black girl
with a small round face
and thick wide glasses.
She waited alone
on the other side of the room
as dancers moved
between us
graceful as small minnows
swimming through blue
shallow waters. I wanted to
wade right into the water
come up and make a big splash for her
on the other side of the room where
she'd stood all night staring
across the vast empty spaces
—as if peering across a big wide sea—
to pull her in up to her knees.
I knew the others would laugh
but so what.
We'd hold each other tight
and slowly wade out farther
until the water lifted us up
and carried us out on a crystal
blue tide of music.

Hot Summer Night in Chicago

Sam Cooke's voice
came from
far away
drifting down our
hot quiet street
in the
dead heat
of that
summer night
which did not
move or stir
through the window.
Listening,
eyes open.
Fully awake.

Working Out at the Corner Lounge
75th & King Drive

Spilling out onto
the quiet streets
the Hammond B
tumbles and
somersaults
followed by a complete
drum set and
red Gibson
hollow-body guitar
and maybe a
funky old
tarnished saxophone
that just happened
to be sitting out
followed by a large
black woman
—dress hiked up
over her brown
padded thighs—
raucously laughing
and spilling out
herself more than just
a little drunk.

Are You Experienced?

He stands
in the middle of the room
only a damp bath towel
wrapped around his flabby
middle-aged waist
bent over a little
hand and arms out
as if playing that sleek new
black-and-white Fender Stratocaster
with the natural hard maple finish on the neck.
The kind Hendrix
played that night 45 years ago
when the lights dimmed and the feedback
from his stacked Marshall amps rose like a
stampeding herd of prehistoric bison
when a lone spotlight shone on him
from behind his wide-brim black hat
as he chimed the first three choruses of
Are You Experienced?
He stands there for a moment
transfixed and blinded in the light
when his daughter walks in
winces at the volume of the stereo
turned all the way up high
looks at him
in just the bath towel
as he plucks down
on imaginary strings
gets embarrassed
averts her eyes
gripes *Oh, Dad,*
Are You Experienced—again?

and quickly leaves the room.
He turns the volume down low
touches the strings gently
like the opening of *Little Wing*
and alone
—by himself—
begins to sing.

The First Lesson of Beauty
to Elizabeth

Never turn
away from
your own beauty.
It may gently
tap you
on the shoulder
one day
and you'll look back
to see a total
stranger and wonder
what she wants of you—
if you're in
her way or just
blocking her view.
Step aside in deference
to let her go by.
Her walk and
form, black curly head of hair
and air will look
just like you
moving farther ahead.
You may
think it an
odd coincidence
that you should
meet someone
so beautifully reminiscent
to have just walked
out of one of your own dreams.
Don't hesitate.

From a distance she'll turn
and suddenly
recognize
you as a long-lost friend.
Go ahead
while she pauses there
a moment
waiting for you
to catch up with her again.

Face the Music

for Reneé

Come on, darlin',
I can't dance that well
and neither can you
and we aren't those young'uns
we were a few years back
and we're a few pounds more
but the hell with that.
I wanted to be an astronaut
or some such thing and you
a First Lady of a President
whose name was John or
Jack—and thinking like that
we probably screwed up our
lives, or at least part of the way.
It looks a whole
lot different than we
thought it was supposed to be.
And we look in a mirror and say
Shit! This isn't what we
were supposed to be,
this isn't it at all.
But hang it and dang it.
I want to kick up a fuss and
hold you tight for one last
whirl across this dark dance floor
'cause we ain't gettin' any younger
and time's flyin' out the side door
and the youngsters will laugh and say,
Look at those old codgers—
what do they think they're doing?
But the hell with them.

Will you take this dance?
The clock is ticking
but it ain't stopped yet
and there's a few minutes left
before the big hand strikes twelve,
so what the hell
what do you say we get up
while the band's still playing our song
just as a condemned man
would whistle along
with the nightingale
singing outside his cell
at dawn
just about when it's time
to get up and face the music.

Jazz Song

Here in the
jazz of late October
I think of you
heavy as the
wetness of leaves
mixed with their
fallen color.
They are suddenly
sodden and hard to
lift from their
flame-colored lethargy.
There are many tones
gone awry today
and seem to float
off-key in gray cloudiness.
The wind is raw, drowsy
as a muzzled trombone
groaning next to a
sweet, unsuspecting piccolo—
but that is the
music of jazz!
It's eat or be eaten
take what is offered
and make of it what you will—
a blithe combining
of light and dark
bone and hair
of white smoke
and dark gristle
that rise from the voice
when it speaks unfettered
in the cold clear air

—mixing the elements—
the seasons
copulating and creating
offspring together
as if such things had bodies
as we too do.

St. Peter, Minnesota: Barry Harris

On this warm fall night
jazz mingles with a
steady southern breeze
drifting through all
these dark and deserted
streets. The rustle of
fallen leaves keeps
perfect time with
the light steady tapping
of my feet.
You came on
late
last night
with the warm
end of September
breezes
deep down in
south-central Minnesota
playing your bebop piano
I'll Always Be Loving You
and I recognized your nod
to the great Bud Powell.

Birth of the Cool: Minnesota

I know, Miles,
you didn't have rural southern Minnesota
in mind when you
blew your classic mute
on your famous *Birth of the Cool*
sessions in New York, circa 1949.
But it's the way the paper-thin
ice forms on the edge of the lake
in late October:
meeting at the cold dark water's edge
—still open and free
though not for long—
with the ripples of these short choppy
muted notes of yours
blown just out of reach
this cool windy autumn morning.

Pure Country

She flags down
this pickup truck.
Inside, a gum-smackin',
hay-balin', tight faded jeans-wearin',
shit-kickin', Tom T. Hall-playin' son of a bitch
pushes his big
ten-gallon Stetson
up from his brow
and says
Honey, you goin' my way?
She looks down
at his diamondback-rattler-snakeskin
cowboy boots and twelve-gauge shotgun
on the rack just in back of his head,
pouch of Red Man on the seat,
open can of Miller High Life
in the plastic cup holder
and says
No, honey, I can pass
on that today
and walks away.
He shouts at her
over Merle Haggard's *White Line Fever*—
Well, honey, you ain't exactly
the pick of the litter yourself
jams his Chevy into gear,
and drives away. His vanity plates,
PRCNTRY, say it all.

Small-Town Blues

Every day I hear
the same jazzy blue songs
in my head—
saddy, sad tunes
down in this small
dusty town.
It does my heart good
to hear them again and again
from hour to hour
as bread dough rises
over my big porcelain bowl.
My husband won't
hear of it when
sudden tears well
up in my eyes.
"What's wrong now!" he shouts.
Nothing, I say, nothing.
I'm just so happy I could cry.
He drives
to the hardware store
the same way he always goes
thinking I'm turning
into a real basket case
keeping quiet about it
until it all goes away.
Never arguing with destiny.
Never testing fate.

Doggone Blues

for Dave Etter

I'd be a doggone fool
not to listen to these doggone blues
in this doggone river town—
jes' a po' white boy
without a doggone friend around
and no doggone home to call my own.

My doggone girl
done picked up and gone—
done picked up and put me down
in this doggone river town.

Yesterday evenin' the doggone train
come down these doggone tracks
black man in boxcar waved at me
and I just waved back
tellin' me, *Be seein' ya soon, son*—
wasn't telling me no doggone lie.

When I heard that doggone train whistle
blow down that doggone line
right then and there knew
I'd be a doggone fool
not to listen to these doggone blues.

Skinny Bird Blues

These skinny birds
all got the blues
empty husks for seeds
and dry bits of leaves
means little or no food.
The fat ones have
all flown south
the skinny ones stay
perched close to
the old empty house.
High above the
deep drifting snow
cold and hungry
with no
place to go.

Poinciana

Somewhere on a hot
and stormy Saturday night
in Kasota, Minnesota,
Poinciana is playing
on the radio
above the kitchen stove.
The electric mixer
is left on and forgotten
as it whips cake batter
all over the walls and floor.
A balding middle-aged man
in just his T-shirt and boxer shorts
and his plump aproned wife
slowdance in dim summer light
as yellow and white daisies
outside in the garden
feverishly shudder
and shake at the sound
of falling rain.

Ko Ko Taylor

Said *Now let me take you down*
into the basement.
And then she started to sing
I cried all night for you!
We slowly took one step down
and then another, a single light bulb
hanging by a frayed cord dangling
from the ceiling.
There was
a damp musty smell
of stored roots, bulbs, seeds
all coated with a thick layer
of coal dust. A big black cast iron
furnace stood
in the middle of the floor—
a fire was burning!

Strollin'

Dexter sometimes seems
to become completely lost
in this melody
—wonderfully so—
Strollin'
here and there
stopping to smell
the red, red roses
with seemingly
no particular place
to go.

For John Lee Hooker
On his 80th birthday

John Lee, I was
within sixty miles
of Clarksdale
on a recent trip
to your home state
of Mississippi,
but couldn't get there.
Happy Birthday, anyway!
Everyone born
in this whole wide world
sometime in their life
has been close enough to Clarksdale
—even if they never quite got there—
to know what the blues are.

Bessie Smith Sings the Blues in Autumn

Her face becomes
frozen hard to it,
stuck forever
in one perfect expression—
eyes closed, mouth open,
head slightly tilted back
toward the sky,
deep furrows
of a freshly plowed field
appearing on her dark brow.
The note she sings,
almost a hymn,
becomes as small and black as
one last leaf in autumn
suddenly blown from a bare
exposed limb.

Prez

Lester's
Sound
Insinuated
That
There
Would
Always
Be
A
Door
Somewhere
That
We'd
Find
Already
Unlocked
If
We
Ever
Tried
To
Open
It.

Art Blakey

Time hovers above us.
Between being an
exact and inexact science
the wide-open spaces
is where I travel,
putting down little markers
for the others to follow.
Call it trail blazing
or putting down footings
deep in the ground
for a foundation
to build a sturdy house upon.
The structure
must be large enough
to include everyone—
all their irreconcilable differences,
the sun and moon, the stars, all.
At the center
there is a groove, a notch
in the universe
where all things
come together
and for a moment,
at least, they all
exist as one.
This is where
the others in the band,
including myself,
follow the beat
of the drum.

Lester Bowie

Today it's dead calm.
A pale white mist
covers this sleepy
southern Minnesota town.
Earlier this morning
golden-yellow bands
of thick clouds spread
one atop the other
across the horizon
like a musical measure
where notes are played,
then erased
and forgotten forever.
This morning, though,
I think of you—
a fade hairdo, wire-rim glasses,
Fu Manchu goatee, and mustache,
a spotless white lab coat,
supine gold lamé necktie—
holding your great golden trumpet
up high to the sky
like Dizzy once used to do
on *Salt Peanuts*
about to blow
that first impeccable note
which suddenly brings the sun up.

The 14th and Final Way of Looking at a Blackbird

John Coltrane's closing chorus of
Bye-Bye Blackbird—
after it's done
is just a tiny dot
fading
on the horizon

Chubby Checker Comes to North Dakota

Oh, yes, I remember
watching Chubby Checker
on our black-and-white TV
dancing The Twist.
A large caramel-colored man
a whirlwind with a perpetual smile
telling us
Come on, baby,
let's do The Twist.
It was like he was telling us
to climb out of our storm cellars
at the height of a terrible thunderstorm
and fling ourselves to the wind.
Even the grandmas and grandpas
who spoke but few words of English
all their lives
thought this an amazing *"think"*—
this America!
Kids like me
we had our dreams, like the real crazy one
I had later that night about
Chubby appearing in town
calling all the young people
together, like Jesus riding into Jerusalem
on a donkey, a bed of palms
strewn in his path,
telling us
Children, you are all now
and forever more free.
He smiled beautifully,
raised his hand as
if giving us a blessing.

We were crying and so happy,
sang like the black Baptist gospel choir
that came here once.
Imagine! White
kids from Napoleon, North Dakota,
who'd never seen a real black person
in their entire lives
singing and dancing in the street
shouting out to our belighted Chubby
We're free at last! We're free at last!
Thank God Almighty, we're free at last!

Giants for All Time
In Memory of S. P. Leary

This is to the memory of S. P. Leary, the great drummer who was part of the legendary Howlin' Wolf Blues Band, which at one time featured Hubert Sumlin, J. T. Brown, and Sunnyland Slim. S.P. died a few days ago, and his passing was gratefully noted on NPR. When I heard the news, I immediately thought back to New Year's Eve 1969. I was a young puppy then, brash enough to fancy myself a budding blues man. My best friend, Rodney, and I went to this Catholic high school gymnasium on the South Side, where Wolf and his band were playing a party. We were devotees and supplicants, prostrate at the knee of the master—and Wolf was a huge, imposing man. A giant, in fact, almost god-like when he strutted and moaned through songs like *Smokestack Lightning*, *Ain't Superstitious*, and *I Asked Her for Water*. His harmonica ranged from come-cry to last dying gasp to lonesome train whistle to wail of a newborn just pulled from its mother's womb. Strangely, he took an instant liking to us, signed his autograph, "Best Wishes, Wolf," on cocktail napkins, and laughed warmly when we said we wanted to play the blues. "It was jes' music when I was you boys' age, jes' our music, we never called it blues." He said he remembered playing for 25 cents a night at sawdust juke joints deep in the Mississippi Delta and picking cotton all day, but insisted, "I'd always pay my way." Later, the great sax player J. T. Brown had too much New Year's cheer and passed out on stage. Wolf fired him on the spot: "J.T., you fired, man," he said, standing over his slumped, motionless body. At the stroke of twelve, Wolf sang *Moanin' at Midnight*. He threw one long arm behind him, where it hung down like a tail between his legs, then got down on all fours and howled like a wolf. In fact, he was a wolf, transformed right before our eyes. Rodney and I glanced at each other. Was this really happening? As Howlin' Wolf slowly rose from beast back to human, it was S. P. Leary's beat—a beat that came from way back, all the way back to the very dawn of time—that delivered him here, now standing tall and completely upright. A giant of a man, for sure. All of them—Hubert, S.P., and Sunnyland. Giants for all time.

Goin' Down Slow

for Larry Wohl

We're riding the Jackson Park/Howard EL, a late Saturday afternoon, and there's a good mix of people on the train—shoppers with their kids, workers getting off the weekend shift, all heading southbound from downtown. At 12th & Roosevelt, an older—very drunken—caramel-colored man weaves on to the train. He's dapperly dressed in a tick-weave gray suit with vest and gray-and-black tie. His clothes, far from cheap, are disheveled, however, and his white shirttail hangs over his pants like a tattered flag of surrender. All the seats are taken, so he stands and holds on to the aisle pole. We watch him lurch forward when the train lurches forward, and backward when the train wheezes to a stop. He spins around like a top when the train leans hard into a sharp corner, and bobs up and down like a paper cup on high waves in Lake Michigan. When his fine felt hat falls to the floor, he tries to retrieve it—like a golfer getting a ball from the cup—and he falls right over onto the floor in a heap. We all watch in amazement as he rights himself, like a gymnast who has fallen off the beam but bravely hops back up to finish the routine. I sense everyone on the train is thinking the same thing I'm thinking: This guy is about to get sick and heave all over. And when he belches loudly, we grit our teeth and close our eyes as if bracing for the imminent impact of a car wreck. But the crisis passes without further murmur, and we sit relieved, though still on guard. A large light-skinned woman dressed in a proper wool suit and carrying a Marshall Field's bag finally asks the man if he'd like to take her seat. He bobs and weaves again and chivalrously but slowly doffs his hat to her and says, "No ma'am, yo' keep yo' seat. This may be Sodom and Gomorrah, and people do all kinds of wicked things without caring much about what they're doin' it for, but I was still raised in the old-fashioned Christian way." Seeming to stare at her large bosom for a time—weaving back and forth while trying to focus, he says, "You can do one kindness for me, Miss, if you will." The woman clearly regrets her offer, but curtly replies, "What?" Without batting an eye, the man breaks into the *Goin' Down Slow Blues*:

Please write my mother and tell her the shape I'm in.
I said to write my mother and tell her the shape I'm in,
tell her to pray for me and forgive me for my sins.

When he stops singing, all eyes on the train are on him. He seems to be waiting for an important question. The train pulls into the 47th Street station, and he turns toward the door without another word and stumbles off. As the train moves on again, everyone seems to exhale one long collective sigh of relief. The large woman adjusts her hat and looks into her Marshall Field's bag to check if everything's still there. Then a laugh rises over the clack of the tracks and spreads through the entire car. Soon everyone is laughing—even the woman, who's now doubled over in her seat, tears welling up in her big sad eyes.

Roadhouse Dance

This guitar is
neither black nor blue
but sounds the shade of twilight
or the tone of darkness
just before sunrise,
does not speak the whole truth
and nothing but
somewhere in between
the truth and nothing but.
Nor is it a pretty flower
that blooms when you
pluck its string but
a garish red petal appears
like dim lights in a roadhouse
and the smell will
bowl you over at the door.
Dark figures in various
positions and poses move
across the floor
and as they move
step together and hold
each other tight and their
coupling dance gives off
a bittersweet fragrance
blossoming well into the night.

When Lester Left Town

for Dave Etter

When Lester left town
the only dry cleaning place
that stretched and pressed shirts
the old-fashioned way
shut down
knee-high weeds
grew up
in the wide deep cracks
on the municipal tennis courts.
The city tore up
Main Street to replace
a busted water line but
then ran out of money
so construction just ground
to a halt
leaving a big black hole
in the center of town.
A man's wife of 32 years
cleaned out their savings account
and took only one suitcase
of clothes and left a note
on the kitchen table
written on the back
of their joint bank statement.
It simply read
I'm outta here!
A black three-legged dog
tried to run a jackrabbit down
and got flattened
out on the blacktop
by a big semi that didn't even stop

to inspect the damage
but just kept going
right on through
like he didn't even see it—
or didn't give a good goddamn
one way or the other
as a cold wind blew
and a colder rain came down
on the day when Lester left town.

A Brief Jazz Who's Who

Adderley, Cannonball (1928–1975)

Alto saxist, multi-instrumentalist. Toured with brother Nat Adderley, Miles Davis, and later as soloist in George Shearing's band in late 1950s. Eventually reformed group with brother.

Allen, Red (1908–1967)

Trumpeter, vocalist, leader, composer. Played with bands in Chicago and New York; active mainly as member of Dixieland-style house band at the Metropole, New York City.

Ammons, Gene "Jug" (1925–1974)

Tenor saxist. Played with King Kolax, Billy Eckstine's big band, Woody Herman, and Sonny Stitt. Spent time recording in New York and playing in Chicago restaurants and clubs.

Armstrong, Louis "Satchmo" "Pops" (1900–1971)

Trumpeter, vocalist. Played in various honky-tonk clubs, dividing his time between St. Louis, New Orleans, New York, and Chicago. Played with other bands and formed his own, including the All Stars, with whom he toured the globe.

Basie, Count (1904–1984)

Leader, pianist, organist. Toured with variety acts in the 1920s, working with artists such as Buster Smith, Don Byas, and Buddy Tate. Appeared in several films in the '40s; played in New York City; continued touring through the '70s.

Blakey, Art (1919–1990)

Drummer. Played with Fletcher Henderson, Billy Eckstine, and the Buddy DeFranco Quartet; leader of the Jazz Messengers.

Bowie, Lester (1941–1999)

Trumpeter, fluegelhorn player, vocalist, leader. One of the organizers of the Association for the Advancement of Creative Music in the 1960s, including Sho' 'Nuff Orchestra, which toured globally.

Byas, Don (1912–1972)

Tenor sax. Led Don Carlos and his College Ramblers; lived in Los Angeles and New York; spent time in Europe playing with Duke Ellington; toured with Jazz at the Philharmonic; soloist in Great Britain; toured Japan with Art Blakey.

Carter, Ron (1937–)

Bassist. Played locally in Michigan and led groups in New York. Used miniature bass (described as mix between cello and full-size bass). Played with the Milestone Jazz Stars and toured nationally.

Catlett, Big Sid (1910–1951)

Drummer, composer. Worked with musicians such as Sammy Stewart, McKenney's Cotton Pickers, Louis Armstrong, and Benny Goodman. Considered one of greatest modern jazz drummers of the 1930s and '40s.

Chambers, Paul (1935–1969)

Bassist. Worked with Benny Green, Joe Roland, J. J. Johnson, Kai Winding, and Miles Davis. Known for exceptional technique and exciting improvisations.

Clayton, Buck (1911–1991)

Trumpeter, arranger. Played with small bands in Los Angeles; leader of Earl Dancer's Band; led own band, The 14 Gentlemen from Harlem; toured globally with own sextet; worked with artists such as Joe Bushkin, Tony Parenti, and Benny Goodman.

Coleman, Ornette (1930–)

Alto saxist, composer. Played with various quartets and in band led by Pee Wee Crayton. Toured in New York, Germany, and Sweden.

Coltrane, John (1926–1967)

Saxist. Considered one of the greatest saxophonists, whose music sparked many disagreements among critics. Worked with artists such as Eric Allan Dolphy, Ornette Coleman, and Miles Davis; formed own quartet as well.

Criss, Sonny (1927–1977)

Alto saxist. Played with Howard McGee and Garland Wilson; led combos during the 1950s; played in clubs in Paris, Germany, and Belgium.

Davis, Eddie "Lockjaw" (1921–1986)

Tenor saxist. Led combos in the 1940s and '50s; toured Europe with Count Basie; also served as soloist and road manager for the Count Basie Band in the '60s.

Davis, Miles (1926–1991)

Trumpeter, leader. Worked with artists such as Charlie Parker, Coleman Hawkins, and Benny Carter; formed the Capitol Band, which incorporated new instruments into jazz.

Desmond, Paul (1924–1977)

Alto saxist. Won *Down Beat* critics poll as best new star on alto sax in 1953; toured in England and the Middle East; known for light sound, clear tone, and hip style; one of the most important alto men of the 1950s.

Dodds, Baby (1894–1959)

Drummer. Praised by Louis Armstrong and Max Roach; played with musicians such as Bunk Johnson, Frankie Dusen, and Lil and Louis Armstrong.

Drew, Kenny (1928–1993)

Pianist, composer. Played with Lester Young and Charlie Parker in the 1950s; formed own group in Los Angeles; spent time in Europe.

Eldridge, Roy (1911–1989)

Trumpeter, pianist, vocalist, fluegelhorn player, drummer. Prominent in development of trumpet jazz in the 1930s; gained fame as featured trumpeter and singer for Gene Krupa's band in the '40s; toured Europe in the '50s with Jazz at the Philharmonic, Ella Fitzgerald, and Oscar Peterson.

Ellington, Duke (1899–1974)

Pianist, arranger, composer. Known for hits including *Solitude, Sophisticated Lady*, and *In a Sentimental Mood*; leader of The Washingtonians; toured nationally and internationally through the early '70s.

Ervin, Booker (1930–1970)

Tenor saxist. Led own groups in United States and toured Europe in the 1960s.

Evans, Bill (1929–1980)

Pianist, leader, composer. Known as one of the most impressive modern pianists; had own combo at age sixteen; won a Grammy for *Conversations with Myself*.

Garland, Red (1923–1984)

> Pianist. Worked with Miles Davis in the 1950s; later formed and toured with own trio.

Gillespie, Dizzy (1917–1993)

> Trumpeter. Strived for swing in the beginning, switched to bop later, and eventually created what became known as bebop. Became sensation in 1945 after forming his first band and touring Europe.

Gonsalves, Paul (1920–1974)

> Tenor saxist. Featured in Sabby Lewis' band in the early 1940s; played with Count Basie, Dizzy Gillespie, and Duke Ellington.

Gordon, Dexter (1923–1990)

> Tenor saxist, composer. Greatly influenced by Lester Young; toured nationally with musicians such as Louis Armstrong, Billy Eckstine, Cee Pee Johnson, and the Three Deuces; played numerous jazz festivals in Europe during the 1960s.

Gray, Wardell (1921–1955)

> Tenor saxist. Worked with artists such as Earl Hines and Count Basie, and in bands with Benny Carter and Billy Eckstine.

Hampton, Lionel (1909–2002)

> Vibraphonist, band leader. Vibraphone's greatest pioneer; worked with almost every top name in jazz.

Hancock, Herbie (1940–)

> Pianist, composer. Known for his great improvisations on the keyboard and a key figure of electronic jazz sound; performs mainly in New York.

Harris, Barry (1929–)

> Pianist, composer. Played in Detroit in the 1950s; worked with Cannonball Adderley, Yusef Lateef, and Coleman Hawkins in the '60s; later led own trio.

Hawkins, Coleman "Bean" (1904–1969)

> Tenor saxist. Known as leader of the tenor saxophone; became great soloist in the 1920s; led own combos and bands during the '40s; played with artists such as Mamie Smith, Fletcher Henderson, Illinois Jacquet, and Duke Ellington.

Hines, Earl "Fatha" (1903–1983)

>Pianist, singer, composer. Known for his originality in jazz piano; led house orchestra at the Grand Terrace Café in Chicago in the 1930s; joined Louis Armstrong's All Stars in 1948.

Hodges, Johnny "Rabbit" (1906–1970)

>Saxist, composer. Worked closely and gained world recognition with Duke Ellington; formed own septet; successful in the R&B market; well known for slow, melodic solos.

Holiday, Billie (1915–1959)

>Singer. Gained international fame after recording with Teddy Wilson's orchestra; toured as a solo performer in the 1940s and '50s; known as a true jazz voice.

Hooker, John Lee (1917–2001)

>Guitarist, vocalist, songwriter. Toured the U.S. and Europe. Played with Eddie Kirkland, Eddie Taylor, Carlos Santana, and Bonnie Raitt. Appeared and sang in The Blues Brothers in the '80s. Played in Memphis, Detroit, and Chicago.

Jacquet, Illinois (1922–2004)

>Tenor saxist, bassoonist, leader. Became celebrity with *Flying Home* with Lionel Hampton's band; performed with Count Basie in the 1940s, then with his own bands.

Johnson, Robert (1898–1937)

>Singer, guitarist. Recognized as one of the best country blues artists; recorded for Vocalion in 1936–37.

Jones, Hank (1918–)

>Pianist, composer. Worked with Ella Fitzgerald; staff musician at CBS; influences include Fats Waller, Teddy Wilson, and Art Tatum; specialized in commercial recording field.

Jones, Jo "Papa Jo" (1911–1985)

>Drummer. Worked with artists such as Ted Adams and Tommy Douglas; spent majority of his time with Count Basie.

Jones, Joe "Philly" (1923–1985)

>Drummer. Known as one of the most dynamic percussionists of the modern school.

Kirk, Andy (1898–1992)

Bass and baritone saxist, leader. Became nationally known with Andy Kirk and His 12 Clouds of Joy with *Until the Real Thing Comes Along*; later recorded in California with new band.

Kirk, Rahsaan Roland (1936–1977)

Tenor saxist, multi-instrumentalist. Occasionally played three instruments simultaneously; toured Europe and performed at various jazz festivals.

Kloss, Eric (1949–)

Saxist, pianist, drummer, composer. Led own groups since 1965; performed at various jazz festivals.

Konitz, Lee (1927–)

Alto saxist. Early experience with commercial bands in Chicago; influenced by Lennie Tristano; refused offers to join many bands or to adapt his style.

Lunceford, Jimmie (1902–1947)

Leader, arranger, multi-instrumentalist. Exhibited high-note trumpet work, a rarity of his time; known for solos; gained fame as leader of the Jimmie Lunceford Orchestra.

McLean, Jackie (1932–2006)

Alto saxist, composer. Worked with various artists through the 1950s; played for Broadway's *The Connection* in 1959-60; toured Japan; taught at Hartt College in Hartford Connecticut.

Mobley, Hank (1930–1986)

Tenor saxist, composer. Worked with artists such as Art Blakey, Max Roach, and Thelonious Monk; influenced by Charlie Parker.

Monk, Thelonious (1917–1982)

Pianist, composer. Gained popularity in the 1950s; featured in quartet with John Coltrane; many Monk compositions have since become jazz standards.

Nelson, Oliver (1932–1975)

Leader, saxist, flutist, arranger. Worked with artists such as Jeter-Pillars, George Hudson, Louis Jordan, and Wild Bill Davis.

Page, Walter (1900–1957)

Bassist, baritone saxist, leader. Influenced greatly by folk and spiritual music he sang with his family as child; played with the Blue Devils (eventually became the Original Blue Devils), Count Basie, Roy Eldridge, and others.

Parker, Charlie "Bird"(1920–1955)

Alto saxist, composer. Co-founder with Dizzy Gillespie of the "bop" movement; one of the most imitated musicians of the 1940s and '50s.

Powell, Bud (1924–1966)

Pianist. Composer. Played with Thelonious Monk, Frank Socolow, Dexter Gordon, J. J. Johnson, Sonny Stitt, Fats Navarro, and Kenny Clarke. Spent time in New York playing with a number of bands, including Cootie Williams'.

Rameriz, Ram (1913–1994)

Pianist, organist, composer. Played with artists such as the Louisiana Stompers, Willie Bryant, and Ella Fitzgerald; toured Europe with Bobby Martin in the 1930s and with T-Bone Walker in the '60s.

Scott, Shirley (1934–2002)

Organist, pianist, trumpeter. Toured with husband, Stanley Turrentine; continued touring after they separated with artists such as Harold Vick and Sweet Basil.

Shorter, Wayne (1933–)

Saxophonist and composer. Played with Art Blakey and the Jazz Messengers, Miles Davis, Horace Silver, Herbie Hancock, Ron Carter, Tony Williams, and Carlos Santana. Formed the fusion group Weather Report with Joe Zawinul. Formed his current band with pianist Danilo Perez, bassist John Patitucci, and drummer Brian Blade.

Sims, Zoot (1925–1985)

Saxist, clarinetist. Freelanced in New York for several years; toured Europe with Benny Goodman; freelanced again in California; inspired by Lester Young; noted for excellent improvisations.

Smith, Jimmy (1925–2005)

> Organist. Known for improvisations and unique tone; formed own trio in the 1950s; toured Europe in the '60s, and later with various artists in New York and Chicago.

Stewart, Rex (1907–1967)

> Cornetist, multi-instrumentalist. Led own band with Sid Catlett, but most notable were recordings with Duke Ellington, which best represented his style.

Stitt, Sonny (1924–1982)

> Tenor, alto, and baritone saxist. Style considered more uniform than artists such as Charlie Parker—but also known as one of the most successful bop alto sax players after Parker.

Tatum, Art (1910–1956)

> Pianist. One of the most famous and imitated jazz pianists since his arrival on the scene in the 1930s; performances with own band, The Three Deuces, led to international fame and touring.

Taylor, Cecil (1933–)

> Composer, pianist. Music demonstrated awareness of the folk heritage of jazz; showed ties to Duke Ellington and Thelonious Monk, but his ideas were original.

Webster, Ben (1909–1973)

> Tenor saxist, pianist. Brought the tenor to full maturity in his music; best remembered for recordings with Duke Ellington in the 1940s.

Williams, John (1909–1954)

> Alto saxist, clarinetist, leader. Worked with artists such as Al Cooper (Savoy Sultans) and Chris Columbus; led own bands in New York and Boston.

Williams, Tony (1946–1997)

> Drummer. Played with Miles Davis Quintet during the 1960s; formed own trio after leaving Davis; toured with Herbie Hancock.

Wilson, Teddy (1912–1986)

> Pianist, arranger. Worked with artists such as Erskine Tate, Louis Armstrong, Billie Holiday, and Benny Goodman; worked for the CBS Orchestra in the 1950s.

Woods, Phil (1931–)

Alto saxist, clarinetist, composer. After studying clarinet at Julliard, played with various artists and toured Europe with Dizzy Gillespie in the 1950s; formed the European Rhythm Machine; leads quintet in New York.

Young, Lester "Prez" (1909–1959)

Tenor saxist, clarinetist. Idolized Frankie Trumbauer; toured with father's band, then led own in the 1920s; toured with The Bostonians and the Count Basie Orchestra; led own groups again in the '40s and '50s.

Compiled with the assistance of Erin Sandburg.

Acknowledgments

I wish to extend deepest gratitude and appreciation to the following people for their help and support, without whom this book would not have come to fruition. Thanks to Joyce Sutphen, Dave Etter, Adrian Louis, David Haynes, and John Calvin Rezmerski. I want to thank the Minnesota State Arts Board; Dean Mariangela Maguire of Gustavus Aldophus College; and the GAC Research, Scholarship, and Creativity Grant for providing support for this project. I also wish to thank The Loft Literary Center in Minneapolis—and especially Jerod Santek and the WIP (Works in Progress) Program—for the opportunity to read and air these poems in public for the first time. Thanks also to Bill Holm (in memory), and The Arts Center of St. Peter, Minnesota.

A very special thanks to Reneé Bryant for doing early and difficult edits, and for shaping these poems as they took form over a number of years.

Some of the poems in this collection have previously appeared in different forms in the following publications: *Blue Island*, Cross+Roads Press; *Where One Voice Ends Another Begins: 150 Years of Minnesota Poetry*, edited by Robert Hedin, Minnesota Historical Society Press; *Stardust and Fate: The Blueroad Reader*, edited by John Gaterud, Blueroad Press; *There is No Other Way to Speak*, edited by Bill Holm, Minnesota Center for the Book Arts; *The Blue Earth Review; Great River Review;* and *North Coast Review.*

Finally, I would like to recognize and thank my colleague, friend, and kindred spirit for all these years, Carolyn Wilkins, for providing the beautiful and soulful music accompanying and underpinning these poems. And, quite naturally, many thanks and sincere gratitude go out to John and Abbey Gaterud of Blueroad Press.

Contributors

Philip S. Bryant

Born and reared on Chicago's South Side, Philip S. Bryant is the author of several collections of poetry, including *Sermon on a Perfect Spring Day*, which was nominated for a Minnesota Book Award in 1999. Most recently, his work appeared in *Where One Voice Ends, Another Begins: 150 Years of Minnesota Poetry*. He has also been published in *The Iowa Review*, *The Indiana Review*, *The American Poetry Review*, and *Nimrod*. Phil was a fellow of the Minnesota Arts Board in 1992 and 1998, and has served on the governing board of The Loft, the premier literary and arts center in the Twin Cities. Bryant is a Professor of English at Gustavus Adolphus College in St. Peter, Minnesota.

Carolyn Wilkins

Jazz pianist and vocalist Carolyn Wilkins has been an active participant in the Boston music scene for more than twenty years as a performer, educator, and composer. A graduate of Oberlin Conservatory and the Eastman School of Music, Carolyn is currently a Professor of Ensembles at Berklee College of Music in Boston. She has released four critically acclaimed albums of original compositions. A swinging pianist and vocalist in the tradition of Diana Krall, Shirley Horne, and Nina Simone, Carolyn's fresh and memorable songs treat subjects as diverse as sex, satire, and spirituality with warmth and humor.

Colophon

Text set in Bembo Std. Today's Bembo typeface was designed by Stanley Morrison for Monotype in 1929. His face is based upon one cut by Francesco Griffo for the Venetian printer Aldus Manutius, who first used it in 1495 in a book for the Italian Cardinal and humanist Pietro Bembo.

Titles set in Futura Std. Designed by Paul Renner between 1924 and 1926, and commercially released in 1927, Futura is based on simple geometric forms. It uses strokes of nearly even weight and eliminates all non-essential elements, making it efficient and straightforward.